Greetings From Chicago

Mary Martin &
Nathaniel Wolfgang-Price

Schiffer Publishing Ltd®
4880 Lower Valley Road, Atglen, PA 19310 USA

Other Schiffer Books by Mary L. Martin

Bathing Beauties of the Roaring '20s. Mary L. Martin & Tina Skinner.
Greetings from New Orleans: A History in Postcards. Mary L. Martin, Tina Skinner
Hawaiian Fish. Mary L. Martin
Hollywood Homes: Postcard Views of Early Stars' Estates. Mary L. Martin, Tina Skinner, & Tammy Ward
Miami Memories: A Midcentury Journey. Mary L. Martin, Tina Skinner, & Nathaniel Wolfgang-Price
Midget Exhibit: Images from the Heyday of Dwarf Display. Mary L. Martin & Tina Skinner
Naughty Victorians and Edwardians: Early Images of Bathing Beauties. Mary L. Martin & Tina Skinner
Cape Cod Memories: An Illustrated History in Postcards. Karen Choppa & Mary L. Martin
Geisha Women of Japan's Flower & Willow World. Tina Skinner, Mary L. Martin, & Wes Ponder
Greetings from Havre de Grace. Craig David & Mary L. Martin
Hawaii Remembered: Postcards from Paradise. Tina Skinner, Mary L. Martin, & Nathanial Wolfgang-Price
Historic Christmas Art: Santas, Angels, Poinsettia, Holly, Nativity, Children, and More Royalty-free Images on CD. Mary L. Martin & Tina Skinner
Historic Holiday Art: New Year, Valentines, St. Patrick's Day, Easter, July 4th, Halloween, & Thanksgiving. Tina Skinner & Mary L. Martin
Lighthouse Views. Tina Skinner, Mary Martin Postcards
Memories of Memphis: A History in Postcards. Ginny Parfitt & Mary L. Martin

Other Schiffer Books on Related Subjects

Advertising Postcards. Robert Reed
Art Deco Architecture: Miami Beach Poscards. Paul Clemence
Birds of Cape Cod & the Islands in Postcards. Roger S. Everett
Cape May Postcards.
Card Photographs: A Guide to Their History and Value. Lou W. McCulloch
Greetings from Ohio: Vintage Postcards 1900-1960s. Robert Reed.
Miami Beach Postcards.
Mies van der Rohe's Farnsworth House Postcard Book. Paul Clemence
Newport News: A Vintage Postcard Tour. Harold Cones & John Bryant

Library of Congress Control Number: 2006925631

Designed by Mark David Bowyer
Type set in Benguiat Bk BT / Humanist 521 BT

ISBN: 0-7643-2545-0
Printed in China

Published by Schiffer Publishing Ltd.
4880 Lower Valley Road
Atglen, PA 19310
Phone: (610) 593-1777; Fax: (610) 593-2002
E-mail: Info@schifferbooks.com

In Europe, Schiffer books are distributed by
Bushwood Books
6 Marksbury Ave.
Kew Gardens
Surrey TW9 4JF England
Phone: 44 (0) 20 8392-8585; Fax: 44 (0) 20 8392-9876
E-mail: info@bushwoodbooks.co.uk
Website: www.bushwoodbooks.co.uk
Free postage in the U.K., Europe; air mail at cost.

Contents

A Little Bit About Chicago

Introduction

In his poem "Chicago," poet and Chicago resident, Carl Sandburg, writes one of the most famous descriptions of Chicago, calling it, "Hog Butcher for the World, / Tool Maker, Stacker of Wheat, / Player with Railroads and the Nation's Freight Handler; / Stormy, husky, brawling, / City of the Big Shoulders" (Sandberg 1916). He goes on to further, praising Chicago for its rough and gritty strength, its bold spirit, and its pride in all its qualities. Sandberg shows Chicago as it is, a city that is vibrant and alive with industry, with transport, and with energy. Connected with the country and the wider world through railroads and waterways, Chicago was well known as a center for finance and industry, as well as being a major transportation hub.

Linked as it was with so many other places in the country and the wider world, it is easy to understand why many people chose to visit Chicago. For some it was the chance to conduct business, to broker a deal, or to purchase the goods that came to Chicago via train and cargo ship; for others it was a stop on a longer journey across the country; for others still it was simply the thrill of visiting a big city, seeing the magnificent skyscrapers and the other sights the city had to offer. Where visitors went, postcards returned; tourists sent back postcards by the dozens, letting their friends and families know where they were, what they saw, how they were doing, and that they had arrived at their destination safely. The pictures on the front and the correspondences on the back of the cards fascinated those "back home" and often inspired them to travel abroad to see the sights printed on the cards themselves. Postcards from the 1900s to the 1950s showcase some of the Windy City's most famous highlights. Quoted material from the back of the postcards is included in the captions, along with historical trivia and present-day facts.

From the back: "Chicago, that wonderful town, wonderful in the sense that it is one of the four largest cities in the world and is growing all the time."

Circa 1940s, $3-4

Greetings from Chicago, Illinois, the "Windy City."

Circa 1940s, $3-4

Chicago was incorporated in 1833. "In little over 100 years, [it] grew from a village of a few log cabins to the fourth largest city in the world."

Cancelled 1941, $3-4

"You can have a Jolly Time in Chicago."

Cancelled 1921, $6-8

History

The city of Chicago had its beginnings back in 1795, when its future site was ceded to the United States following the Northwest Indian War. Though the land itself was mostly prairie bogs and marshland, it nonetheless attracted a fair amount of pioneers who settled down and began to build a town. The settlers named their city "Chicago," which was derived from *Checagou*, the Potawomi word for "skunk" or "wild onion," referring to the smell given off by the surrounding marshland and by the wild leeks that grew there.

When it was incorporated in 1833, Chicago encompassed an area of three-eighths of a square mile and was home to a population of 350. In 1837, the state of Illinois granted Chicago a city charter. Not long after that the population boomed, rising to 4,000. By 1857, the population had risen to 9,000 people, making Chicago the largest city in the Northwest.

The completion of the Illinois and Michigan Canal and the arrival of the Galena & Chicago Union Railroad in 1848 heralded the beginning of a new facet of Chicago's identity. Connected by land and by water to various points around the country and the world, the city soon gained a reputation as a major transportation hub. With the boats and trains came industries and banks, which increased the city's wealth and encouraged further growth.

Chicago's fortunes continued to increase until 1871, when tragedy struck the blooming city. At nine o'clock at night, on Sunday October 8, 1871, firefighters responded to a fire that had broken out on the city's Southwest Side.

Popular legend states that the fire was started by a cow, owned by Patrick and Catherine O'Leary, kicking over a lantern. Recent research has suggested, however, that it was either Daniel "Pegleg" Sullivan or Louis M. Cohn who actually started the fire. The legend about the cow was made up by a reporter who thought it would make a more interesting story.

Regardless of how it started, the fire did begin at 137 DeKoven Street in a barn owned by the O'Learys. Fed by the drought-dried wood of the surrounding buildings and encouraged by a steady wind blowing from the southwest, the fire soon moved beyond the O'Learys' property, spreading northeast until it burned itself out twenty-four hours later. Three hundred people died in the fire and among the 300,000 survivors, 100,000 were left without homes. The fire decimated the downtown business district, destroying 18,000 buildings as well as a number of small business and private homes.

Though it is remembered as one of the worst disasters in Chicago history, the Great Chicago Fire, in some ways, proved to be a benefit to the city. Plans to implement a radical redesign of the city, which had been stalled before the fire, could proceed without any opposition. The fire also contributed to the implementation of strict new fire safety codes and led to the preference of fireproof materials by Chicago builders, which led to the use of steel framed buildings and the development of the skyscraper. The rebuilding and modernization benefited the city as a whole, bringing it up to the same level as more modern cities like New York City.

Rebuilt and modernized, Chicago continued on its path of growth and expansion. In 1893, Chicago was chosen over New York City, Washington D.C., and St. Louis as the site for the World's Columbian Exposition, celebrating the 400th Anniversary of the discovery of the New World by Christopher Columbus.

Buoyed by the attention drawn by the Exposition, Chicago moved into the new century confident in itself and its self-image. The railroads and waterways continued to bring in passengers and cargo, further benefiting the city's economy and image. In 1927, the city's first airfield, the Chicago Municipal Airport (later renamed Midway Airport in honor of the Battle of Midway) opened, further enhancing Chicago's reputation as a hub of cross-country transportation.

Today Chicago is still known as the cultural, financial, and transportation capital of the American Midwest and is ranked as one of the ten most influential cities in the world by the Globalization and World Cities Study.

A bird's-eye view of Michigan Avenue, showing the Wrigley Tower and the London Accident Insurance Building.

Cancelled 1927, $6-8

An aerial view of the Outer Drive Link Bridge and the skyline of the city.

Circa 1940s, $4-6

A nighttime view of the Water Tower. The Palmolive Building is visible in the background.

Cancelled 1932, $3-5

Chicago businessman Potter Palmer built this castle on Lake Shore Drive for his wife Bertha in 1885, leading to the establishment of the elite Gold Coast neighborhood.

Circa 1920s, $5-7

The Chicago skyline as seen from Chicago Harbor. Sights like the Wrigley Building and the Merchandise Mart are visible.

Cancelled 1941, $4-6

The Marine Room of the Chicago Historical Society Building was an adaptation of the Peabody Museum's Robinson Hall.

Circa 1940s, $8-10

In Honor of....

Like every other city, Chicago has its share of monuments, memorials, and public sculptures and is well-known for these public displays of art. Some of the first monuments erected in Chicago were war monuments in the city's cemeteries, dedicated to the men from Chicago and Cook County who had fought in the Civil War. In the city's lakefront parks, epic bronze statues were also erected to commemorate heroes like Ulysses S. Grant and George Washington.

After World War I, the style of monuments shifted, emphasizing the concept of "living monuments," which would be beneficial to the community and serve not just as reminders of influential individuals but as valuable community resources. For example, the Elk's War Memorial, which honors the soldiers who died in World War I, also houses the offices of the Elk's National Grand Lodge.

This monument of George Washington is located in Washington Park, which is also named after him.

Cancelled 1908, $3-4

Monument dedicated to Alexander Hamilton, the first secretary of the United States Treasury.

Circa 1930s, $5-6

This memorial to Ulysses S. Grant was dedicated in 1891 and is located in Lincoln Park. There is also a monument of Abraham Lincoln located in Grant Park.

Cancelled 1905, $3-5

Located on Lake View Avenue and Diversey Parkway, the Elk's War Memorial is dedicated to the members of the Elks who died in World War I.

Cancelled 1943, $3-5

The Elks War Memorial was built in 1926 and cost $3 million to build. It also houses the Elks' National Grand Lodge offices.

Circa 1920s, $3-4

City Sights

Public Buildings

One of the city's first public buildings, the Chicago Courthouse, was built in 1835 on the corner of Clark and Randolph Streets. Like many public buildings built during this time period, the Courthouse was built in Greek revival style.

As the city's population grew, the need for larger public buildings grew as well. A second, larger City Hall and Courthouse building was built in 1853. Many of Chicago's early public buildings were built in the downtown section of the city and were subsequently destroyed in the Great Chicago Fire.

After the Fire, the city of Chicago wanted a new public building that would declare to the world that Chicago had recovered and was thriving once again. The design selected was one by a city architect named James J. Egan. Unfortunately, the new building took twelve years to complete and was plagued with structural problems and difficulties caused by poor interior planning, which made it hard to work in.

Between 1906 and 1911 a new structure was built, which still serves as the Chicago City Hall and the Cook County Offices today.

Occupying a square city block, the City Hall and County Building is home to the government offices for the City of Chicago and Cook County, Illinois.

Cancelled 1924, $3-4

The new Chicago Post Office was built by the Federal Government, "to handle the enormous mailing requirements of Chicago's business houses."

Cancelled 1950, $2-3

A glimpse of the interior of the rotunda and dome of the new post office building.

Circa 1915, $5-7

The Chicago Public Library, the Newberry Library, the Harper Memorial Library, and the John Crerar Library, Chicago's "four leading Libraries."

Cancelled 1943, $5-6

The Chicago Public Library is home to a circulating library of 382,280 books and nearly two million books each year are loaned out for home use.

Circa 1920s, $4-5

Another view of the Chicago Public Library. The library building was built in 1897.

Cancelled 1911, $3-7

The Washington Street Staircase, inside the Chicago Public Library.

Cancelled 1911, $6-7

Streets

In 1830, the City of Chicago commissioned James Thompson, a cartographer from southern Illinois, to create the city's first official map. Instead of naming the streets according to their destination, which was the common practice at that time, Thompson chose to name the streets after important local and national figures.

The tradition continued as the city grew; however, rapid urban growth, the annexation of local communities, and the heavy use of street naming as a political favor began to create confusion with multiple streets having the same name and streets being known by several different names.

A building superintendent, Edward P. Brennan, suggested a solution to the problem in 1901. He suggested that the city should be ordered as a grid with a uniform street numbering system with State and Madison Streets serving as the primary North-South and East-West axes. The system was officially adopted by the city in 1908 and implemented in 1909.

The tradition of naming city streets after important figures still continues, with the most popular source of street names being local real estate developers, followed by English towns, and former city mayors and aldermen.

A crowd of excursionists gather at the Rush Street Bridge waiting to board the steamers at the docks just below. In the spring and summer months, the Rush Street Bridge was one of the most congested spots in the city.

Circa 1915, $8-9

A view of Madison Street looking east from Dearborn Street.

Cancelled 1913, $6-8

Crowds of shoppers and pedestrians make their way up and down the sidewalks on State Street.

Circa 1915, $8-10

The Corner of State Street and Madison Street, "The Busiest Corner in the World."

Cancelled 1924, $7-8

A postcard shot of North State Street looking south from Lincoln Park.

Cancelled 1909, $5-7

The corner of State and Madison Streets was the center of the loop retail districts. A number of department stores were located here.

Circa 1915, $9-12

A nighttime view of State Street.

Cancelled 1912, $8-10

Another view of State Street.

Cancelled 1906, $7-9

State Street, "the busiest street in the City. It is crowded with shoppers by day and sightseers by night."

Circa 1915, $5-7

The State Street Bascule Bridge.

Cancelled 1911, $8-9

A bird's-eye view of Wacker Drive as seen from the top of the Merchandise Mart.

Circa 1940s, $3-5

Wagons line Haymarket and West Randolph Street.

Circa 1915, $9-12

A view of La Salle Street showing the Chicago Board of Trade Building in the background.

Circa 1940s, $2-3

Running parallel to the Chicago River, Wacker Drive consists of a lower drive for commercial traffic and an upper drive for car and pedestrian traffic.

Cancelled 1929, $6-8

Lake Shore Drive and Oak Street Beach looking north towards Lincoln Park.

Circa 1940s, $5-7

Overlooking Lake Michigan, Lake Shore Drive was home to a number of Chicago's wealthy residents.

Circa 1915, $6-8

Lake Shore Drive and North Avenue.

Circa 1920s, $4-6

Lake Shore Drive runs along the eastern side of Lincoln Park.

Cancelled 1921, $5-6

An aerial view of Lake Shore Drive and Oak Street Beach. Also visible are the Drake Hotel, the Palmolive Building, and the McKinlock Campus of Northwestern University.

Circa 1950s, $5-6

One section of Lake Shore Drive was nicknamed the "Gold Coast" and was, at one time, the second-wealthiest urban neighborhood in the United States.

Cancelled 1919, $4-6

The elevated railroad bridge at Van Buren Street.

Circa 1915, $8-10

The Van Buren Street Viaduct.

Cancelled 1912, $8-10

From the back: "The greatest produce market in the world is located on South Water Street."

Cancelled 1907, $10-12

Found on Chicago's South Side, Michigan Boulevard is one of the connecting streets for some of Chicago's parks.

Cancelled 1909, $6-8

Looking north on Ashland Boulevard.

Cancelled 1910, $6-8

Only eight blocks long, South Water Street runs along the south side of the Chicago River.

Circa 1915, $10-12

Drexel Boulevard, a part of Chicago's residential section.

Cancelled 1915, $6-8

Michigan Avenue, "perhaps the best known of Chicago's many famous thoroughfares."

Circa 1940s, $2-3

63rd and south Halsted Streets, "the busiest corner on the South side."

Circa 1915, $9-12

Another aerial view of Michigan Avenue, this one looking north from the Chicago River.

Circa 1940s, $2-4

A view of Michigan Avenue from Lake Michigan. The small building on the lakeshore is the Chicago Yacht Club.

The Michigan Avenue Link Bridge. The bridge weighed 10,000 tons and was built to ease transportation along the riverfront.

Cancelled 1929, $5-7

Shoppers peruse the stalls along Maxwell Street.

Cancelled 1943, $8-10

Some of the famous buildings along Michigan Avenue.

Cancelled 1910, $6-8

Located on Roosevelt Road and 14th Street, the Ghetto Market was in a neighborhood of Chicago inhabited primarily by Russian Jews.

Circa 1940s, $7-9

The Outer Drive Bridge connects the north and south outer drives along Lake Michigan, making it possible for traffic to travel from one side of the city to the other without undue delays.

Cancelled 1942, $5-7

At the time it was built, the Outer Drive Bridge was the world's largest double deck bascule bridge.

Circa 1940s, $5-7

This bridge carries the Lincoln Park section of Outer Drive over the channel that leads to the Diversey Lagoon.

Circa 1920s, $5-7

Looking northwest along Milwaukee Street, Irving Park, and Cicero Avenue.

Circa 1940s, $5-7

A view of Adams Street, looking east from State Street.

Cancelled 1907, $10-15

Skyscrapers

The skyscraper in Chicago came about as a direct result of the Great Chicago Fire. As wooden buildings had contributed to the spread of the fire, the city's new fire codes favored masonry buildings over wooden ones. Unfortunately, the ground around the lakes, where most of the buildings had been destroyed, was too soft and swampy to support large masonry buildings. At the time, masonry buildings were built using load-bearing walls, a style of construction in which the weight of the entire building is supported by the structure's walls. In areas with soft soil, this method was impractical, as the weight of the structure pressing down on the walls would cause the building to slowly sink into the ground. The solution was presented by a group of architects now known as the First Chicago School. Instead of the weight being supported by the load-bearing walls, it would be supported by an interior framework of iron and steel I-beams and girders; the buildings could still be tall but would weigh less and could be built in places where the ground was soft and not be in danger of sinking or collapsing. The buildings would also be made of fireproof materials, which made them doubly attractive to fire-cautious builders and developers. It was this new design, known as a "skyscraper," that allowed Chicago to prosper in the years following the fire, helping the city become the metropolis it is today.

The first skyscraper built in Chicago was the Home Insurance Building. It was built in 1885 and was ten-stories tall.

An aerial view of Chicago, "City of Towers."

Circa 1920s, $5-7

The London Guarantee and Accident Company Building, the company's American headquarters, was built on former location of Fort Dearborn.

Circa 1920s, $3-5

The interior of the Harris Trust and Savings Bank.

Cancelled 1913, $6-8

The Corn Exchange National Bank.

Cancelled 1910, $5-7

The lobby of the People's Gas Building.

Circa 1915, $5-7

The south tower of the Wrigley Building was finished in 1921 and the north tower in 1924. The Wrigley Building was the first office building in Chicago to have air-conditioning.

Circa 1915, $5-7

Built by the estate of department store founder Marshall Field, the Field Building is 530 feet tall.

Circa 1940s, $2-3

The Wrigley Building was built in the 1920s by William Wrigley to house the head-quarters of his chewing gum company.

Circa 1920s, $4-6

Situated on North Wacker Drive, the Civic Opera Building is 567 feet high with a 20,177,080 cubic foot interior.

Circa 1940s, $2-3

Another view of the Field Building.

Cancelled 1944, $2-3

The home of the Chicago Civic Opera, the Civic Opera Building houses a 3,400 seat auditorium.

Circa 1940s, $2-3

Built in 1869, the Chicago Water Tower was one of the few structures downtown to survive the Great Chicago Fire.

Circa 1940s, $2-3

The Lindbergh Beacon on top of the Palmolive Building could be seen by aviators as far east as Cleveland and as far south as St. Louis.

Circa 1940s, $2-3

The Water Tower was built as part of a water pumping system that drew fresh water from Lake Michigan.

Cancelled 1912, $5-7

The corridor of the Straus Building Tower Observatory. From the top of the Observatory a person can see as far away as Wisconsin.

Circa 1915, $6-8

The Travel and Transport Building.

Cancelled 1933, $5-7

The Daily News Building is twenty-five stories tall and houses the plant, the business, and the editorial departments for the *Daily News* and the studios for WMAQ.

Circa 1940s, $2-3

Thirty-two stories tall, the Continental Companies Building was one of the tallest buildings on Michigan Avenue.

Circa 1940s, $2-3

The design of the Tribune Tower was the result of an international contest held by the *Chicago Tribune* to design "the most beautiful office building in the world."

Circa 1920s, $5-7

The Tribune Building is twenty-three stories high and topped with a 140-foot tower.

Circa 1920s, $5-6

Hospitals

In its original charter, the city of Chicago had no legal mandate requiring it to care for the poor when they became ill. Cook County did operate an almshouse in the city, but it was a public charity caring for the poor, the mentally ill, and the disabled as well as the sick and was not a true general care hospital. The city charter did have a provision to guard against infectious diseases and, in 1843, it built an institution devoted to medical care. The institution was located in what would later become Lincoln Park and was meant more to keep those with contagious diseases away from the general population than it was to treat them.

The first general hospital was built in the 1840s. It was a joint venture, with Rush College supplying the doctors, Cook County providing the medicine, and the city itself picking up the tab for the rent. However, the facilities soon proved inadequate to house and treat the number of patients that were admitted and was soon forced to close.

In 1850, Rush College, Cook County, and the City of Chicago opened a new hospital (Illinois General Hospital of the Lakes) in the old Lake House Hotel. It operated along the same lines as the previous hospital had, with the Roman Catholic order of the Sisters of Mercy providing the nursing care. In the spring of 1851, the Sisters of Mercy took over the administration of the hospital, which was renamed Mercy Hospital. Today, Mercy Hospital is the oldest continually running hospital in Chicago.

"Equipped with the very latest hospital facilities," Wesley Memorial Hospital was located on E. Superior Street.

Circa 1940s, $2-3

Like its counterparts in other port cities, the Chicago Marine Hospital was established to care for injured or sick merchant marine sailors.

Cancelled 1909, $5-7

The new Cook County Hospital was built on the site of the old Administration Building on Harrison Street and cost $3 million to build.

Circa 1920s, $4-6

Founded in 1850, Mercy Hospital was one of the first hospitals to be built in Chicago.

Cancelled 1935, $4-6

The Frances E. Willard National Temperance Hospital.

Cancelled 1909, $5-7

The Student Nurses' Dormitory at Ravenswood Hospital.

Circa 1940s, $2-4

The Chicago branch of the Pasteur Institute.

Cancelled 1909, $5-7

Churches

One of the first houses of worship in Chicago was a log cabin built in 1831, opposite Wolf Point, near the Chicago River. The cabin was built by a Methodist congregation, the descendents of whom still worship in the Chicago Temple.

Before that, in 1683, the area had been home to a small settlement of French Jesuits who established a mission, the Mission of the Guardian Angel, in 1696. However, both the settlement and the mission were abandoned long before the Chicago area became part of the United States of America.

As the city grew, the number and variety of churches grew along with it. New ethnic groups arrived in the city from other parts of the United States and other parts of the world, bringing their own ways of worship. Some of these new groups built churches in the parts of the city they settled, while others joined already established congregations. In fact, the construction of a house of worship was one of the sure signs that a congregation was well established.

Today Chicago is home to one of the largest Roman Catholic archdiocese in the United States, as well as a large number of Protestant churches, Jewish synagogues, Muslim mosques, Sikh gurdwaras, and Hindu and Buddhist temples.

"The world's tallest church," the Chicago Temple has occupied the same site on Clark and Washington Streets for the past 108 years.

Cancelled 1947, $2-3

The Temple, itself, is twenty-one stories high with a 140-foot tower at the top. Only the first two stories were used by the church, the rest were offices.

Circa 1920s, $3-4

The Sanctuary for the Chicago Temple could accommodate 1,200 worshippers and people from close to thirty states attended services there each Sunday.

Circa 1915, $6-8

The Eighth Church of Christ Scientist is home to one of the oldest African-American Christian Science congregations in the country.

Circa 1915, $5-6

The Church of Our Lady of Sorrows.

Circa 1915, $5-6

The Chicago Woman's Temple.

Circa 1915, $5-6

Fourth Presbyterian Church moved to its present location on North Michigan Avenue and Delaware Place in 1914.

Cancelled 1949, $3-4

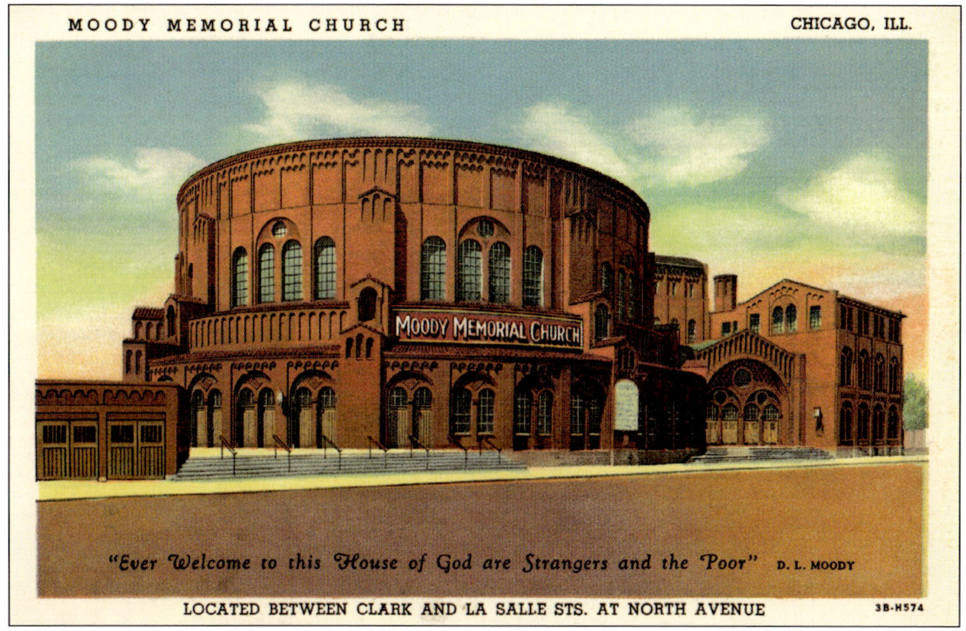

The Moody Memorial Church was founded by D.L. Moody, one of the most famous evangelists of the nineteenth century. He began his evangelical career by starting a Sunday school for underprivileged children in Chicago.

Circa 1940s, $3-4

The First Christian Science Church, 40th Street and Drexel Boulevard.

Circa 1915, $5-7

Located on North State and Superior Streets, the Cathedral of the Holy Name was "within walking distance from the loop."

Cancelled 1917, $2-3

Built in 1875 to replace the Cathedral of Saint Mary, the Cathedral of the Holy Name is the mother church of the Archdiocese of Chicago.

Circa 1940s, $2-3

The St. James Episcopal Church is an example of the eighteenth century style church architecture found throughout the Midwest.

Circa 1940s, $2-3

The Corpus Christi Church is "one of the finest churches in Chicago and is situated in the most beautiful part of the city, near the entrance to Washington Park.

Circa 1920s, $3-5

The Woodlawn Park Presbyterian Church.

Circa 1915, $5-7

St. Jarlaths Church on Jackson Boulevard and Hermitage Avenue.

Circa 1920s, $3-5

St. Matthias Church found on Ainslie Street and Claremont Avenue.

Circa 1940s, $2-3

Known as "The Country Church of the City," Granville Avenue Methodist was a popular venue for weddings.

Circa 1920s, $3-4

Railroads

A large part of Chicago's reputation as a hub of transportation comes from the city's connection with the railroad. The first railroad in Chicago was the Galena & Chicago Union Railroad, chartered in 1836 to build tracks from Chicago to the lead mines in Galena, Illinois. Not long after, other railroad companies came to Chicago and built lines connecting the city with other parts of Illinois and with Wisconsin. Other railroads linked Chicago with cities like Detroit, Cincinnati, New Orleans, Cleveland, Omaha, St. Louis, St. Paul, and Kansas City. A number of these railroads also maintained yards, shops, and headquarters in the city as well.

The railroads were particularly important in moving grain, livestock, and freight, which contributed to three of the Chicago's other major industries, meatpacking, grain marketing, and freight handling. Some local companies also manufactured supplies for the railroad, including freight cars, passenger cars, and diesel engines.

Currently Chicago is considered the most important railroad center in North America and the most important interchange point for freight traffic between major railroads. It has more lines of track that radiate from the city in more directions than any other North American city and is second behind New York City in its daily volume of commuter traffic.

In 1874, a number of railroad companies came together and made an agreement to build a union station (a station where the tracks and facilities are shared by more than one railroad company) on land owned by the Pennsylvania Railroad Company. The construction for the station was finished in 1881.

Cancelled 1910, $7-9

The new station was built on South Canal and Adams Street on the west side of the Chicago River.

Cancelled 1906, $8-10

The current Union Station opened in 1925 and was built by the Union Station Company.

Cancelled 1928, $6-8

The Ticket Lobby in Union Station was situated between the Main Waiting Room and the Train Concourse. It was considered by many to be an "unusually attractive" space.

Circa 1920s, $8-9

At the time of its construction, Union Station was one of the largest railroad stations in the world, serving as a passenger terminal for the Pennsylvania Railroad, the Chicago, Burlington & Quincy Railroad, the Michigan Central Railroad, the Chicago and Alton Railroad, and the Chicago, Milwaukee & St. Paul Railway.

Circa 1930s, $5-7

The Fred Harvey Lunch Room at Union Station could seat close to six hundred people.

Cancelled 1927, $8-9

A view of Northwestern Depot, as seen from the Wells Street Bridge.

Circa 1915, $7-9

The terminal of the Chicago and Northwestern Railway on Madison Street.

Cancelled 1949, $3-5

A track elevation stretching across 16th and Clark Street.

Cancelled 1909, $8-10

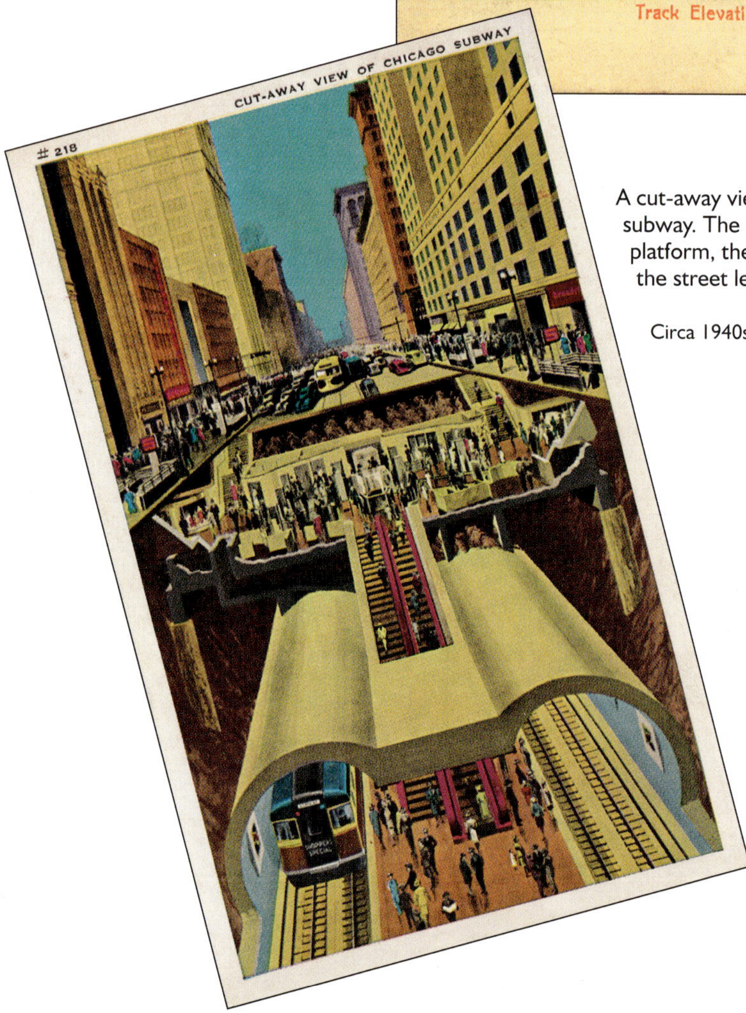

A cut-away view of a typical Chicago subway. The main tubes, the center platform, the escalators, mezzanines, and the street level entrances are all visible.

Circa 1940s, $7-8

The Illinois Central Depot, the main station for the Illinois Central Railroad.

Circa 1915, $6-8

Grant Park, the Illinois Central Depot is visible in the background.

Cancelled 1910, $5-7

Opened in 1885, the Dearborn Station is one of the oldest train stations in Chicago.

Circa 1920s, $6-8

Union Stock Yard

Carl Sandberg, in his poem "Chicago," called Chicago "Hog Butcher for the World," which referred to its thriving meatpacking industry. From the Civil War to the 1920s, Chicago was the largest meatpacking center in the United States.

At that time, Chicago was in the unique position of being between the livestock farmers in the Midwest and the large urban meat markets on the East Coast, and having the railroad connections between the two.

Unfortunately, there was no easy way to get the livestock from the railroad to the packing plants. Cattle and hogs often had to be driven through the streets to get them from one place to the other. To solve this problem, a group of the leading meatpacking and railroad companies came together to form the Union Stock Yard and Transit Company in 1860. Five years later, on Christmas Day in 1865, the company opened Union Stock Yard, a 475-acre complex located south of the city proper on Exchange and Halstead Streets.

By the middle of the 1870s, most of the major meatpacking companies had moved to the area surrounding the stockyards and by the end of the century it was the most successful industrial park in Chicago.

Union Stock Yard remained open for over a hundred years, until finally closing on August 1, 1971. Of the stockyard structures, only the limestone gates remain standing. These gates were designated a city landmark in 1972.

The Dexter Pavilion at the Union Stock Yard.

Cancelled 1910, $8-10

Union Stock Yard opened on Christmas Day in 1865 and stayed open for close to 106 years before closing in 1971.

Cancelled 1939, $5-7

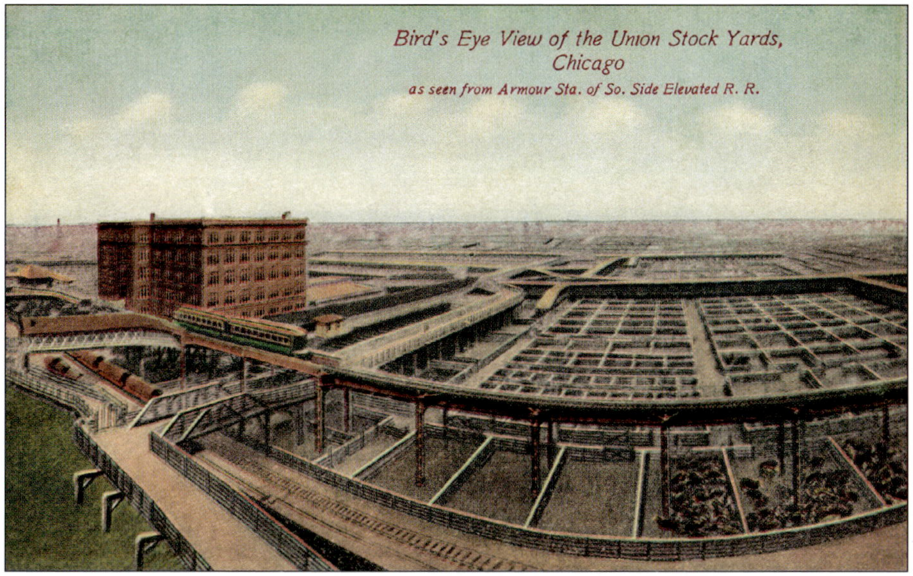

A view of the Union Stock Yard as seen from the South Side Elevated Railroad's Armour Station.

Circa 1915, $6-9

The Union Stock Yard started on the South Side at 37th Street and extended south for five hundred acres.

Circa 1920s, $6-7

Close to 1,000 cars of livestock from twenty-two states arrived and nearly $2 million worth of livestock was sold at Union Stock Yards each day.

Circa 1940s, $5-6

Stores

The first store in Chicago was founded in the 1780s by Jean Baptiste Pointe du Sable, a Haitian immigrant who was also the first non-Native American to settle in the area. Du Sable established a trading post out of his home, where he dealt with European trappers, members of the local Potawatomi tribe, and traders from back East.

Long after du Sable had sold his trading post, a dry-goods merchant, Marshall Field, along with his partner Levi Leiter, opened a massive dry goods store occupying an entire block on State Street. The store, renamed Marshall Field & Company after Field bought out his partner, would go on to become one of Chicago's largest retailers and one of the largest department stores in the world. It was the first department store to have a sit-down restaurant and, as a result, was an important social destination as well as a place to shop. The company was also responsible for building the Merchandise Mart, also located in Chicago, which still claims to be the world's largest commercial building.

Chicago was also home to two of the country's largest mail-order companies, Montgomery Ward & Company and Sears, Roebuck & Company. Montgomery Ward was founded in Chicago in 1872, after salesman Aaron Montgomery Ward began to convince people in the rural Midwest to buy dry goods like hardware, furniture, and clothing through the mail. The concept soon proved to be very popular, particularly when Ward initiated a "satisfaction guaranteed or your money back" policy. Sears, Roebuck moved to Chicago in 1895. Both companies took advantage of Chicago's railroads to send catalogues and ship orders.

Montgomery Ward & Company was founded in Chicago in 1872 by Aaron Montgomery Ward, a former traveling salesman. It was the world's first mail order business.

Cancelled 1909, $5-7

Marshall Field & Company also got their start in Chicago.

Cancelled 1915, $6-8

The Marshall Field's Store on State Street first opened in 1879 to replace the previous store, which was destroyed in the Great Chicago Fire.

Cancelled 1909, $6-8

A corner in the Grill Room – Marshall Field's was the first department store to open a sit-down restaurant inside one of its stores.

Cancelled 1912, $6-8

The main aisle on the first floor in Marshall Field's Store for Men – this store was in a separate building from the main store and was opened in 1914.

Circa 1920s, $5-7

The Tiffany Mosaic Dome in Marshall Field's was the first ceiling to be built with favrile iridescent glass.

Circa 1915, $6-8

The women's petticoat section in Marshall Field's.

Circa 1915, $7-9

A view of the Linen Section, the Bric-a-brac Room, and the Tea Room inside Marshall Field's.

Circa 1915, $10-12

One of Marshall Field's advertising concepts was to publish postcards with pictures of the various sections inside the store. Pictured here are the Oriental Rug Section, the Indian Goods Section, and the Flag Section.

Circa 1915, $10-12

Some exterior shots of Marshall Field's.

Circa 1915, $10-12

Marshall Field's was also the first American department store to open a buying office in Europe.

Circa 1915, $10-12

Other stores, like Siegel Cooper & Company, were also located on State Street.

Circa 1915, $5-7

Built by Marshall Field & Company, the Merchandise Mart cost $30 million and is billed as the "world's largest building."

Cancelled 1941, $5-6

Located on the north bank of the Chicago River, the Merchandise Mart housed several hundred mercantile concerns and the broadcast office of the news station WMAQ.

Circa 1940s, $2-3

The Rothschild & Company Department Store on State Street.

Circa 1940s, $2-3

Clubs

Chicagoans have started and joined clubs and organizations from almost the time of the city's founding. Ethnic clubs, like the Polish National Alliance, quickly formed amongst the city's immigrant population in order to help new arrivals to acclimate to the new society and culture, learn important new skills, and create a network of support as well as helping to preserve cultural traditions. Religious denominations formed organizations like the Walther League for charitable reasons and to provide services for their own members. Improvement organizations formed around neighborhoods to welcome new residents and to work towards solving community problems. Social clubs formed around common interests and activities or just as a place to spend some time with friends. Politically minded citizens of Chicago formed clubs around political parties and causes. Fraternal organizations like the Freemasons, the Elks, and the Oddfellows were also active among the city's middle and upper classes. Health and fitness clubs were also popular among the business and social elites of Chicago. These clubs existed not only to encourage their members to keep active and be physically fit, but were also places to encourage business and social networking. Today, organizations like these and others still play a large role in influencing the lives of individuals throughout the city and are an integral part of the culture and history of Chicago.

The cocktail room at the Edgewater Yacht Club, the "most distinctive cocktail room in America."

Circa 1940s, $2-3

A panoramic view of the South Shore Country Club.

Circa 1915, $5-7

The Kenwood Club.

Circa 1915, $5-7

The main entrance to the South Shore Country Club.

Cancelled 1915, $5-7

Not just for working out, clubs like the Illinois Athletic Club were places where the business elite of Chicago could meet, network, and make deals.

Cancelled 1912, $6-8

The Calumet Club on Calumet Street.

Cancelled 1910, $6-8

The home office building of the Polish National Alliance: Chicago has a large Polish population and is currently home to the largest ethnically Polish population outside of Poland.

Circa 1940, $2-3

Allerton House, the Chicago Club's residential building. There were six floors for women, fifteen for men, facilities for handball, tennis, and the world's largest indoor golf course.

Circa 1920s, $3-5

The Medinah Athletic Club was open only to Masons.

Circa 1915, $3-4

The headquarters of the Walther League, the Lutheran Youth Building was built out of Indiana limestone and was located on the city's North Side.

Circa 1940s, $2-3

Business offices occupied eighteen of the twenty-two floors of the United Masonic Temple; the rest were devoted to Masonic business.

Circa 1940s, $3-4

University of Chicago

The University of Chicago was founded in 1890 by oil tycoon and philanthropist John D. Rockefeller. The University, however, has always dated its founding as July 1, 1891, when its first president was inaugurated. A "self-made man," Rockefeller chose Chicago as the location for the university because he believed that talent and merit rather than family connections should influence education and the acceptance of a university's students. Chicago was far enough away from the bastions of American aristocracy on the East Coast for Rockefeller's belief to become a reality. The founding of the University of Chicago also reflected a need for schools that would focus not only on classical education but also on issues important to the needs of the growing nation.

Following a German model, the university was first set up around a number of graduate institutions and the school remained small compared to its older and more established kindred in the East well into the twentieth century.

Perhaps one of the most famous events to occur at the University of Chicago happened on December 2, 1942, when the world's first self-sustaining nuclear reaction was achieved at the university as part of the top-secret Manhattan Project. Currently the University encompasses 211 acres in Hyde Park.

Oil baron and philanthropist, John D. Rockefeller, founded the University of Chicago in 1890. It opened two years later in 1892.

Circa 1915, $10-12

A panoramic view of the University of Chicago, the Main Campus is located eight miles from the Loop and occupies 211 acres.

Circa 1920s, $6-8

Hull Gate and the Botany Pond.

Circa 1915, $5-7

Hull Court. The University's biological research buildings were once centered around this location.

Circa 1940s, $2-3

Hull House, a dormitory named after Charles J. Hull.

Cancelled 1906, $5-7

The Ryerson Physical Laboratory.

Circa 1915, $5-7

Kelly, Beecher, and Foster Halls, the Women's Dormitories. The University of Chicago was one of the first major universities to allow women to enroll.

Circa 1920s, $4-5

The tower of the Theological Seminary was erected as a tribute to Victor Fremont Lawson, who was a friend and benefactor of the Seminary.

Circa 1940s, $2-3

A gift from John D. Rockefeller Jr., the International House was home to five hundred foreign and American students.

Circa 1940s, $2-3

Another view of Hull Court, this one showcasing the Hull Anatomy Building.

Circa 1915, $5-7

The tallest building on campus, the Rockefeller Memorial Chapel is a memorial to John D. Rockefeller.

Cancelled 1946, $2-3

The Chapel can seat close to 2,000 people and cost roughly $2 million to build.

Circa 1920s, $3-5

The Physiology and Anatomy Buildings of the University of Chicago's Pritzker School of Medicine.

Cancelled 1910, $5-7

Founded in 1895 by Dr. Joseph B. De Lee, the Chicago Lying-In Hospital is affiliated with the University of Chicago.

Circa 1940s, $2-3

The Law Building, Haskell Museum, and Divinity Hall of the University of Chicago. The Law Building was modeled after the King's Chapel in Cambridge, England.

Cancelled 1910, $5-7

Both the Kent Laboratory and Kent Theatre were donated to the University by Sidney A. Kent.

Cancelled 1928, $3-4

A closer view of the Kent Laboratory.

Circa 1920s, $3-5

Cobb Hall.

Cancelled 1910, $5-7

The University of Chicago's Educational Building.

Circa 1915, $5-7

The William Rainey Harper Memorial Library is located on the southern end of the University grounds.

Cancelled 1948, $2-3

With a seating capacity of 1,400, Mandel Hall is the University's main lecture hall and auditorium.

Circa 1940s, $2-3

The Albert Merritt Billings Hospital and the Max Epstein Clinic were the University's general medical units and were the center of the school's medical research and teaching facilities.

Cancelled 1945, $2-3

Schools

Chicago is home to a number of educational institutions. The public schools are run by the Chicago Public School District, which oversees 600 public elementary and secondary schools. It is the third largest school district in the United States, with a student population of 400,000.

The city is also home to Northwestern University, another of the country's top schools, and the University of Illinois, both the city's largest school and one of the largest public universities in the United States. There are twelve accredited theological schools located in Chicago, including the Chicago Theological Seminary, which is the oldest institution of higher learning in the city.

The Academy of Our Lady, at 95th and Throop Streets.

Cancelled 1923, $2-4

The Main Wing of the Chicago Baptist Missionary Training School.

Cancelled 1941, $4-5

The North Division High School, located on the city's North Side.

Circa 1915, $5-7

Found on North Halsted Street, the McCormick Theological Seminary was affiliated with the Presbyterian Church.

Cancelled 1910, $5-7

The Chicago Normal College.

Circa 1915, $5-7

DePaul University and Church on Webster Avenue.

Cancelled 1909, $5-7

Englewood High School.

Circa 1915, $5-7

Lake View High School overlooking Lake Michigan.

Cancelled 1906, $5-7

The Nicholas Senn Technical High School had facilities for over 3,000 students and cost $1 million to build.

Cancelled 1926, $3-5

Built in the early 1920s, the Nicholas Senn Technical High School was "thoroughly modern and absolutely fireproof."

Circa 1915, $5-7

Located on the grounds of Loyola University, the Madonna Della Strada (Our Lady of the Way) Chapel was designed by Andrew Rebori, who was also from Chicago.

Circa 1940s, $2-3

The Chicago Theological Seminary's Thorndike Hilton Memorial Chapel.

Circa 1930s, $3-4

An ecumenical seminary affiliated with the United Church of Christ, the Chicago Theological Seminary enrolls over two hundred students from close to twenty different denominations each year.

Cancelled 1912, $5-7

Northwestern University's Abbott Hall was completed in 1940 and is capable of housing up to 1,000 students.

Circa 1940s, $2-3

The Art Institute of Chicago was founded in 1866 by a group of artists who wanted to open an art school with its own gallery.

Circa 1915, $4-6

A pair of lion statues stand guard at the entrance to the Art Institute.

Circa 1940s, $2-3

After the Great Chicago Fire, the Art Institute was rebuilt and opened its doors to students in 1893.

Cancelled 1941, $2-4

Hyde Park High School, situated on the south side on 62nd Street, Stony Island, and Harper Avenues.

Cancelled 1920, $5-7

Crane Technical High School, 2245 W. Jackson Boulevard.

Circa 1920s, $4-6

Visiting Chicago

Lake Michigan

Lake Michigan is one of the five Great Lakes of North America. Surrounded by Michigan, Illinois, Indiana, and Wisconsin, it is the only one of the Great Lakes that is completely within United States territory. The lake itself is 307 miles long, 118 miles wide, has a surface area of 22,300 square miles, and is 923 feet at its deepest point. It is the largest freshwater lake in the United States and the fifth largest lake in the world.

Chicago is located at the southwestern tip of Lake Michigan, a location that has played an important part in the city's development and growth. In 1848, the Illinois and Michigan Canal was completed, connecting Lake Michigan with the Mississippi River, allowing ships from United States ports on Lake Michigan, and even from Canada, to travel from Lake Michigan to the Mississippi River, and eventually the Gulf of Mexico. It was this canal, along with the railroad, which helped establish Chicago's reputation as a transportation hub. Today, the Chicago Sanitary and Ship Canal is the primary connection between the Mississippi River and Lake Michigan.

Most of the lakefront in Chicago is built up with developments, harbors, or seawalls. The few beaches in Chicago are very popular with residents and tourists and the city imports fresh sand each year to keep them open.

A view of the Loop, bordered by the Chicago River on one side and Lake Michigan on the other.

Cancelled 1942, $2-3

Windsor Bathing Beach on Lake Michigan, as seen from 75th Street.

Cancelled 1910, $6-8

Manhattan Beach: The beaches along Lake Michigan are known for their "squeaking sand," which makes a squeaking noise when trod on due to its high quartz content.

Cancelled 1906, $5-7

Over a mile long, North Avenue Beach is part of Lincoln Park.

Circa 1940s, $2-3

Fishing off the North Shore Breakwater in Lake Michigan.

Cancelled 1909, $5-7

Used for docking lake boats, the Navy Pier had three deck levels for both freight and passenger traffic.

Circa 1930s, $3-4

The Recreation Building on the Navy Pier featured a concert and a dance hall.

Circa 1940s, $2-3

The Municipal Pier's name was changed in 1927 to the Navy Pier to honor the members of the United States Navy who served in World War I.

Circa 1920s, $5-6

The Entrance to Navy Pier: The Pier was part of a plan for two piers to be built on the edge of Lake Michigan. The second pier was never built.

Circa 1920s, $5-6

The East Towers on top of the Recreation Building.

Cancelled 1919, $5-6

Over 3,000 feet long and 292 feet wide, the Navy Pier was one of the longest piers in the country.

Cancelled 1921, $5-6

A Day in the Park

At present the Chicago Park District operates 547 parks totaling 7,300 acres; however, this was not always the case. The first parks in Chicago were tiny pieces of land given or sold to the city by real estate developers in the hopes that the parks would increase the value of the properties they were trying to sell.

It was concern for the public health of the citizens that finally convinced the city of the need of public parks. A physician named John H. Rauch had discovered that the city's water supply had been contaminated by the poor burial conditions of the North Side cemetery near Lake Michigan. In 1860, Rauch's findings, backed by a crusade led by the doctor, convinced the city of Chicago to set aside sixty acres on the North Side, which included the cemetery (the contents of which would eventually be moved to another location), for use as a public park. In the late 1860s, the citizens of Chicago once again campaigned for additional parks. This campaign prompted the State Legislature to establish the West, South, and Lincoln Park Commissions in 1869. The Lincoln Park Commission worked to further develop Lincoln Park (the sixty acres granted in 1860). The West Park Commission worked with architect, engineer, and landscape designer William Le Baron Jenney, to design, lay out, and construct the three parks that are known today as Humboldt, Garfield, and Douglas Parks. Working with Frederick Law Olmstead and Calvert Vaux, the South Park Commission created Jackson and Washington Parks, and Midway Plaisance. As the city grew and annexed more of the surrounding towns, more and more parks were added to the city, with a new commission formed to oversee each individual park. In 1934, the twenty-two independent park commissions were merged into one organization, the Chicago Park District, which still continues to maintain and oversee the city's public parks.

Various scenes in Chicago's Parks.

Circa 1940s, $3-5

The South Entrance to Garfield Park.

Cancelled 1910, $6-8

Children splash around in the McKinley Park swimming pool.

Cancelled 1903, $6-8

The Lily Pond and Pavilion in Douglas Park. Douglas Park begins on west 12th Street and extends for 182 acres.

Circa 1920s, $3-5

The Douglas Park Conservatory.

Cancelled 1910, $5-7

Originally Central Park, Garfield Park was renamed in 1881 in honor of President James A. Garfield.

Circa 1920s, $4-6

A pergola offers shade for hot visitors to Garfield Park.

Cancelled 1916, $3-5

Looking towards Garfield Park on Jackson Avenue.

Circa 1915, $5-7

The Garfield Park Lake was created during the park's construction as a means of draining the construction site.

Circa 1915, $3-5

A later addition to the park, the Garfield Park Administration Building was built in the 1920s.

Cancelled 1942, $2-3

Concerts were given in the Garfield Park bandstand in the summer. The grounds around the bandstand were set up so that thousands of park visitors could find space to sit.

Cancelled 1945, $2-3

The Garfield Park Conservatory is said to be one of the largest conservatories in the world.

Circa 1915, $5-7

A glimpse inside the Garfield Park Conservatory.

Circa 1920s, $3-4

The lagoon and boathouse in Lincoln Park.

Circa 1915, $5-7

Located at the Center and Clarke Street Entrance to Lincoln Park, the Chicago Academy of Sciences was open year-round.

Cancelled 1918, $4-6

Another view of the Chicago Academy of Sciences.

Cancelled 1909, $5-7

Built in stages between 1890 and 1895, the Lincoln Park Conservatory consists of four distinct halls, each featuring a specific type of plant.

Circa 1940s, $2-3

The High Bridge in Lincoln Park.

Circa 1915, $5-7

The Lincoln Park Conservatory is known throughout Chicago for the beautiful flowers growing inside the building and in the surrounding grounds.

Cancelled 1904, $5-7

The Lion House was a major attraction in Lincoln Park Zoo. A large number of different feline species were housed there, many of which were captured abroad by big game hunters.

Circa 1940s, $3-4

A bear cub, like the one pictured here, was the first animal bought for the Lincoln Park Zoo.

Cancelled 1905, $5-7

Visitors to the Lincoln Park Zoo pause to watch the antics of the inhabitants of the Seal Grotto.

Cancelled 1904, $5-7

The Sunken Gardens in Humboldt Park as seen from the edge of the Pergola.

Circa 1915, $5-7

A tranquil pastoral scene in Humboldt Park: The park is named for Baron Freidrich Heinric Alexander Von Humboldt, a famed German naturalist, scientist, and explorer.

Circa 1915, $3-4

From the back: "Humboldt Park is known as the most beautiful of Chicago's West Side Parks."

Cancelled 1940, $2-3

The Lily Pond in Humboldt Park.

Cancelled 1905, $5-7

The largest park on the West Side, Humboldt Park has a total area of 206 acres.

Circa 1920s, $2-4

Parkgoers congregate in front of the Refectory in Humboldt Park.

Cancelled 1912, $6-8

A view of the Humboldt Park Refectory from the park lagoon.

Cancelled 1908, $5-7

A quiet day on the Humboldt Park lagoon.

Circa 1915, $5-7

Humboldt Park was laid out by William Le Baron Jenney, an architect who is best known for being "the father of the skyscraper."

Circa 1915s, $5-7

Another view of the Humboldt Park Refectory, which also doubled as a boathouse and casino.

Cancelled 1910, $5-7

A couple pause to enjoy the scenery in Humboldt Park.

Cancelled 1912, $5-7

Grant Park was named after Ulysses S. Grant, eighteenth President of the United States.

Circa 1915, $5-7

Located at the end of Randolph Street, the pergola in Grant Park "is one of the many beautiful monuments which makes this park a pleasing and harmonious link in Chicago's wonderful park system."

Circa 1920s, $4-6

Kate Buckingham presented the Buckingham Fountain to the city in memory of her late brother, Clarence.

Circa 1940s, $2-3

Colored lights illuminate different parts of the Buckingham Fountain. The fountain is modeled loosely after the Fountain of Versailles in France.

Cancelled 1951, $2-4

A number of famous bands and orchestras have given concerts in Grant Park.

Cancelled 1946, $4-6

Another view of "the Worlds most beautiful plaza" in Grant Park.

Cancelled 1939, $2-3

The two drives pictured here lead into Grant Park from Michigan Avenue.

Cancelled 1953, $5-7

The Jackson Park Sanitarium.

Circa 1915, $6-8

Japanese houses on the Wooded Island in Jackson Park.

Cancelled 1909, $5-7

The Japanese Garden is one of the two structures left in Jackson Park from the World's Columbian Exposition in 1893.

Circa 1940s, $2-3

The Republic Statue in Jackson Park is a smaller replica of a statue built for the World's Columbian Exposition.

Circa 1920s, $3-5

Jackson Park is home to 107 acres of artificial lakes.

Circa 1920s, $3-5

La Rabida, one of Jackson Park's lagoons, as seen from beside the lifesaving station.

Cancelled 1912, $7-8

Parkgoers stroll along the beach in Jackson Park.

Cancelled 1908, $5-6

Jackson Park was laid out by Frederick Law Ohmstead, the same landscape architect who designed New York's famous Central Park.

Circa 1915, $5-7

Forty-six nations participated in the World's Columbian Exposition held in Jackson Park. After the Exposition, a number of the buildings built for it were taken over by the park.

Circa 1915, $7-8

A different view of the German Building in Jackson Park.

Cancelled 1906, $6-7

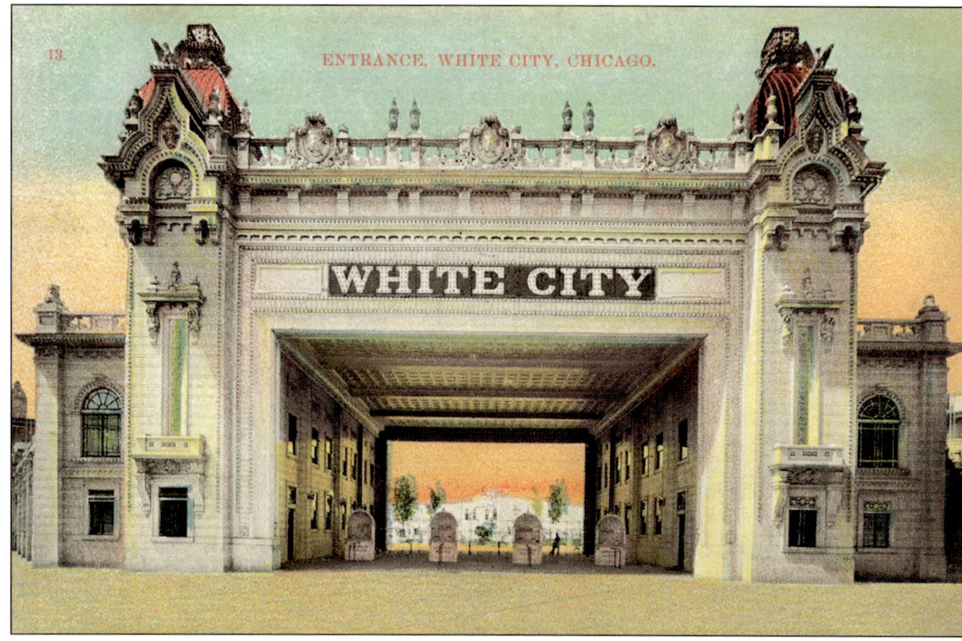

The entrance to White City, "one of the most noted summer amusement resorts in the city."

Cancelled 1909, $8-10

The West Board Walk in White City.

Circa 1915, $8-10

White City was particularly spectacular at night when it was illuminated by thousands of electric light bulbs.

Cancelled 1909, $7-9

White City was built on the South Side of Chicago. The entrance to the park was located on South Park Avenue and East 63rd Street.

Circa 1915, $5-7

The Chutes, one of the many rides and amusements found in White City.

Circa 1915, $7-9

The Dancing Pavilion and Tower at the far end of White City.

Cancelled 1911, $5-7

A typical Saturday at White City Amusement Park.

Circa 1915, $8-10

Named after George Washington, Washington Park was also designed by Frederick Law Ohmstead.

Circa 1915, $6-8

The entrance to Washington Park at 69th Street and Cottage Grove.

Cancelled 1928, $5-7

Like a number of other urban parks at the time, Washington Park was home to a conservatory and sunken garden.

Cancelled 1914, $5-6

Hotels and Restaurants

The first hotel in Chicago was built in 1831, when Mark Beaubain built a frame addition onto his log tavern creating the Sauganash Hotel. As the city grew, the size and number of the hotels inside the city grew as well, spurred on by the rapid physical and economic growth. Hotels like the Tremont House, the Sherman House, and the Metropolitan House offered all the latest in modern conveniences and luxuries like elevators, gas lighting, and steam heat. However, like so many other buildings, the Great Fire destroyed the majority of these hotels. After the Fire, the size and number of hotels changed again as the city grew and rebuilt. Modeled after the palazzo-style hotels found back East, hotels like the Grand Pacific, the Palmer House, the Sherman House, and the Tremont continued the work of their predecessors by offering the latest luxuries in elegant surroundings. After the construction revolution caused by the skyscrapers, Chicago hotels evolved even further, changing into the big luxury hotels of today; hotels like the LaSalle, which was the first of these new hotels to be built in the Loop.

In 1835, the dining room of the Lake House Hotel, serving oysters imported from the East Coast, was the first in the city to offer formal dining with toothpicks, napkins, and menu cards at each table. Conscious of the city's rough and gritty image, Chicago's fine dining restaurants continually sought to advertise their Continental atmosphere and menus, comparing themselves to the best restaurants found in established metropolises like New York City. Union Stock Yards ensured that there was an ample supply of fresh beef readily available and the abundance of railroads and freight cars meant a steady supply of imported oysters and lobsters. In the early twentieth century, a general trend favoring the "exotic" saw these same restaurants expanding their menus by hiring Italian and Chinese chefs. Chicago's high immigrant population also contributed to the restaurant industry, providing chefs for fine dining restaurants, opening restaurants of their own featuring ethnic cuisine, and introducing foods that would eventually becomes staples in Chicago's diet.

The Morrison Hotel, home of the "historic Boston Oyster House and Terrace Casino."

Circa 1940s, $2-3

The Louis XVI Dining Room at the Hotel La Salle. Chicago was well known for the quality of its cuisine. A number of hotels and dining spots would often showcase their dining rooms on picture postcards.

Circa 1915, $7-9

The Stevens Hotel, one of the several fine hotels located on Michigan Avenue.

Cancelled 1926, $5-6

The Stevens also had the benefit of being near enough to the Loop to be convenient for shopping and business but far enough from it to be away from all the noise and traffic.

Circa 1930s, $2-4

The Boulevard Room in the Stevens Hotel was home to the largest hotel ice rink in the country and was a popular nightspot.

Circa 1930s, $6-8

The Hotel La Salle's East Room.

Circa 1915, $7-9

The Buffet in the Hotel La Salle.

Circa 1915, $7-9

The Main Lobby in the Hotel La Salle.

Circa 1915, $7-9

The Blue Fountain Room, named for the distinctive blue fountain located in the center of the room.

Circa 1915, $7-9

The garden of the Hotel Windermere.

Cancelled 1909, $5-7

Located inside the Loop, the Hotel Sherman was "undoubtedly one of the most famous hotels in the United States."

Circa 1940s, $3-4

The Winthrop Terrace Hotel.

Cancelled 1942, $4-6

Hotel Eastgate, "Just a whisper from the Loop."

Circa 1940s, $2-3

The first Palmer House was built by Potter Palmer as a wedding present to his wife Bertha. It opened on September 26, 1871, and burned down in the Great Chicago Fire thirteen days later. It was rebuilt on the same site not long after.

Circa 1915, $6-8

Between 1924 and 1927, the Palmer House was modernized and rebuilt. The reconstruction was done in stages so the hotel would not have to close down and lose any business.

Cancelled 1946, $3-4

The Palmer House's Victorian Room.

Cancelled 1943, $3-4

The Oriole Room and the Cafeteria at the YMCA Hotel in Chicago.

Cancelled 1942, $3-5

An exterior view of the YMCA Hotel: The hotel operated on the same principle as a normal YMCA building, but was open to men, women, and families.

Circa 1940s, $3-5

The furnishings in the Marine Room at the YMCA Hotel were designed by members of the hotel staff.

Circa 1940s, $5-6

Taken from Grant Park, this view shows the Congress Hotel and its annex.

Cancelled 1909, $7-8

The Japanese Tea Room inside the Congress Hotel.

Cancelled 1912, $7-9

Inside the Congress Hotel's Restaurant.

Circa 1915, $7-8

The spacious Banquet Hall at the Congress Hotel.

Circa 1915, $7-8

A number of Chicago hotels, like the Congress Hotel and the Auditorium Hotel, pictured here, booked so many guests each year that they needed to build an annex to accommodate them all.

Cancelled 1908, $5-6

The Hotel Atlantic's Lobby on Clark Street and Jackson Boulevard.

Circa 1920s, $7-8

The Drake, located on Chicago's famous Magnificent Mile.

Circa 1940s, $3-4

As one of Chicago's premier hotels, the Drake has had many prestigious guests over the years, including Winston Churchill, Joe DiMaggio, Marilyn Monroe, and Elizabeth Taylor.

Circa 1920s, $3-4

An aerial view of the Drake Hotel: The Drake had eight hundred guest rooms and room to seat five thousand people in the hotel dining room.

Circa 1920s, $4-6

An apartment hotel, like the Seville on Sheridan Road, was ideal for visitors to Chicago who were planning to stay in the city for more than a few days.

Circa 1920s, $4-6

As its name implies, the Chicago Beach Hotel was located near the beach and Lake Michigan.

Circa 1920s, $5-7

The lobby of the Great Northern Hotel.

Circa 1915, $6-8

Built in 1916, the Edgewater Beach Hotel was near Lincoln Park and Lake Michigan.

Circa 1915, $6-8

Potted flowers brighten the entrance to the Edgewater Beach Hotel.

Circa 1915, $5-7

The West Lounge at the Edgewater Beach Hotel.

Circa 1930s, $5-7

Along with the Drake, the Blackstone was considered one of Chicago's premier hotels.

Cancelled 1914, $6-8

The Edgewater Beach Apartments were built in 1927 as part of the Hotel's complex. This is the only building of the Edgewater Beach Hotel that remains standing.

Cancelled 1928, $5-7

Named for the founder of the Union Stockyards, Thomas B. Blackstone, the Blackstone Hotel was completed in 1910 and opened that same year.

Circa 1915, $6-8

The Blackstone was particularly popular with U.S. presidents and featured a special presidential room.

Circa 1915, $6-8

The Blackstone's Michigan Avenue Entrance.

Circa 1915, $6-8

In 1920, Warren G. Harding was selected as the Republican presidential candidate at the Blackstone, even though the Republican Convention was officially being held at the Coliseum.

Circa 1915, $6-8

The Lobby at the Hotel Lorraine on Wabash Avenue and Van Buren Street.

Circa 1915, $6-8

The Chicago YMCA Building.

Cancelled 1907, $6-8

The Harriet Hammond McCormick Memorial Residence, a YMCA residence.

Circa 1930s, $4-6

Costing $2,750,000, the Victor F. Lawson YMCA had facilities to accommodate 725 men along with the latest physical, educational, and health equipment.

Cancelled 1940, $4-6

Henrici's, Chicago's "most famous restaurant."

Circa 1915, $6-8

The Mandarin Restaurant featured both American and Chinese food and was located on Randolph Street.

Cancelled 1941, $8-10

Places to See

Besides the freight, grain, manufacturing, and meatpacking industries, the railroad also benefited the tourist trade. Passengers traveling by train between the East and West Coasts would frequently change trains in Chicago and spend the time between arrival and departure sightseeing around the city, and the city had plenty for them to see.

The contributions of wealthy businessmen like Max Adler, John G. Shedd, and Marshall Field led to the establishment of institutions like the Adler Planetarium, the John G. Shedd Memorial Aquarium, and the Field Museum – institutions that were highly valued by the citizens of Chicago as well as tourists. Sports teams like the Chicago Bears, Cubs, and White Sox were well known throughout the country and it was not uncommon for visitors to Chicago to attend a game at Soldier Field, Wrigley Field, or Comisky Park.

Chicago's central location in the continental United States, its accessibility, large gathering places, and the ample number of hotels in the city, has also contributed to another of the city's main industries, conventions. As early as 1847, political, professional, industrial, sports, religious, and commercial conventions have been held in Chicago. Large events like the World's Columbian Exposition in 1893 and the Century of Progress Exposition in 1933 saw millions of visitors flooding the railways, occupying hotel rooms by the dozen, and filling up venues like Jackson Park, Soldier Field, and the Coliseum. Ever politically minded, Chicago has been the frequent host of the Republican Party's National Convention ever since the Convention of 1860, when Abraham Lincoln was nominated to run for president.

Construction of the John G. Shedd Memorial Aquarium was finished in 1929 and the first exhibits were opened in 1930. The funds to build the aquarium were donated to the city by John G. Shedd, the president of Marshall Field & Company.

Circa 1920s, $5-6

The second largest indoor aquarium in the United States, the John G. Shedd Memorial Aquarium can hold up to five million gallons of water and twenty thousand fish.

Cancelled 1928, $5-6

The funds for the Adler Planetarium were donated by Max Adler, a philanthropist and businessman from Illinois, as a gift to the city.

Circa 1940s, $2-3

One of the first scientific museums in the country, the Field Museum of Natural History was opened in the late 1800s. It was renamed the Chicago Museum of Natural History in the 1950s and '60s, but eventually returned to its original name.

Cancelled 1949, $2-3

The Adler Planetarium was the first planetarium built in the Western Hemisphere and today is the oldest one still in existence.

Circa 1940s, $2-3

Originally located in Jackson Park, the Field Museum was moved to its new location on Lake Shore Drive in 1921.

Circa 1920, $3-5

Stanley Field Hall in the Field Museum of Natural History.

Cancelled 1924, $4-6

Another sample of the enormous collection owned by the Field Museum.

Cancelled 1908, $7-8

Opened for the 1933 World's Fair, the Museum of Science and Industry is housed in the building formerly occupied by the Field Museum of Natural History.

Circa 1930s, $3-5

Municipal Grant Park Stadium was renamed Soldier Field in 1925 and was dedicated to the American soldiers who died in past wars.

Circa 1930s, $5-7

An aerial view of Soldier Field, showing the Field Museum of Natural History in the background. The field has hosted a number of athletic and sporting events; however, the Chicago Bears did not make the stadium their official home until 1971.

Circa 1920s, $4-6

Standing 105 feet high and capable of seating 13,000 people, the Coliseum was used for a number of shows, exhibitions, and political conventions.

Circa 1920s, $5-7

The Coliseum was built in 1899 on Wabash Avenue by Charles Gunther. It took the place of a Confederate prison that Gunther had shipped from Virginia and had planned to reconstruct in Chicago.

Cancelled 1910, $5-7

With a seating capacity of 25,000 people, the Chicago Stadium was one of the largest indoor sports arenas in the world.

Cancelled 1944, $3-4

Before it was demolished in 1973, the Regal Theatre was a center for the performing arts, particularly among Chicago's African-American population.

Cancelled 1941, $4-6

The view from the stage of the Strand Theatre on Wabash Avenue.

Circa 1920s, $5-7

Like the Coliseum, the International Amphitheatre was the location of a number of conventions and exhibitions held in Chicago.

Cancelled 1953, $3-5

Occupying one quarter of a city block in Tribune Square, this building was the broadcast headquarters for W-G-N Studios.

Cancelled 1940, $3-4

Bibliography

Bachrach, Julia Sniderman. "Park Districts." *The Electronic Encyclopedia of Chicago*. Chicago: The Chicago Historical Society, 2005. http://www.encyclopedia. chicagohistory.org/pages/955.html. 2/14/06.

Berger, Molly M. "Hotels." *The Electronic Encyclopedia of Chicago*. Chicago: The Chicago Historical Society, 2005. http://www.encyclopedia.chicagohistory.org/pages/603.html. 2/14/06.

Buelow, Paul. "Hospitals." *The Electronic Encyclopedia of Chicago*. Chicago: The Chicago Historical Society, 2005. http://www.encyclopedia.chicagohistory.org/pages/602.html. 2/14/06.

"Chicago, Illinois." http://en.wikipedia.org/wiki/Chicago%2C_Illinois. 2/14/06.

Hudson, John C. "Railroads." *The Electronic Encyclopedia of Chicago*. Chicago: The Chicago Historical Society, 2005. http://www.encyclopedia.chicagohistory.org/pages/1039.html. 2/13/06.

Karamanski, Theodore J. "War Monuments." *The Electronic Encyclopedia of Chicago*. Chicago: The Chicago Historical Society, 2005. http://www.encyclopedia. chicagohistory.org/pages/1315.html. 2/13/06.

King, Bruce. "Restaurants." *The Electronic Encyclopedia of Chicago*. Chicago: The Chicago Historical Society, 2005. http://www.encyclopedia.chicagohistory.org/pages/1066.html. 2/14/06.

Kotlowitz, Alex. *Never a City so Real*. New York: Crown Journeys, 2004.

Lowe, David Garrard. "Public Buildings in the Loop." *The Electronic Encyclopedia of Chicago*. Chicago: The Chicago Historical Society, 2005. http://www.encyclopedia.chicagohistory.org/pages/1019.html. 2/13/06.

Pacyga, Dominic A. "Union Stock Yard." *The Electronic Encyclopedia of Chicago*. Chicago: The Chicago Historical Society, 2005. http://www.encyclopedia.chicagohistory.org/pages/2218.html. 2/14/06.

Poe, Tracy N. "Foodways." *The Electronic Encyclopedia of Chicago*. Chicago: The Chicago Historical Society, 2005. http://www.encyclopedia.chicagohistory.org/pages/470.html. 2/15/06.

Reif, Janice L. "Clubs." *The Electronic Encyclopedia of Chicago*. Chicago: The Chicago Historical Society, 2005. http://www.encyclopedia.chicagohistory.org/pages/2465.html. 2/14/06.

Sandberg, Carl. "Chicago." *Wikipedia*. http://en.wikipedia.org/wiki/Chicago_(poem). 2/10/06.

Sawislak, Karen. *Smoldering City: Chicagoans and the Great Fire, 1871-1874*. Chicago: University of Chicago Press, 1995.

Sokol, David M. "Art, Public." *The Electronic Encyclopedia of Chicago*. Chicago: The Chicago Historical Society, 2005. http://www.encyclopedia.chicagohistory.org/pages/80.html. 2/13/06.

"University of Chicago." *Wikipedia*. http://en.wikipedia.org/wiki/University_of_Chicago. 2/14/06.

Wade, Louise Carroll. "Meatpacking." *The Electronic Encyclopedia of Chicago*. Chicago: The Chicago Historical Society, 2005. http://www.encyclopedia.chicagohistory.org/pages/804.html. 2/14/06.

Wakeford, Michael Paul. "Street Naming." *The Electronic Encyclopedia of Chicago*. Chicago: The Chicago Historical Society, 2005. http://www.encyclopedia. chicagohistory.org/pages/1205.html. 2/13/06.

Wilson, Mark R. "Mail Order." *The Electronic Encyclopedia of Chicago*. Chicago: The Chicago Historical Society, 2005. http://www.encyclopedia.chicagohistory. org/pages/779.html. 2/14/06.